© D. C. Thomson & Co., Ltd., 1982
ISBN 0 85116 265 7

The
Fireside Book

*A picture and a poem
for every mood
chosen by*

David Hope

Printed and Published by
D. C. THOMSON & CO. LTD.,
185 Fleet Street, London EC4A 2HS.

SO SWEET LOVE SEEMED

SO sweet love seemed that April morn,
　　When first we kissed beside the thorn,
So strangely sweet, it was not strange
We thought that love could never change.

But I can tell—let truth be told—
That love will change in growing old;
Though day by day is naught to see,
So delicate his motions be.

And in the end 'twill come to pass
Quite to forget what once he was,
Nor even in fancy to recall
The pleasure that was all in all.

His little spring, that sweet we found,
So deep in summer floods is drowned,
I wonder, bathed in joy complete,
How love so young could be so sweet.

Robert Bridges

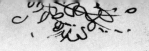

DOG DAYS

WE used to go for lengthy walks into the
  nearby wood,
Where he would let me off the lead, as all good
  masters should.
And he would stroll, and I would stroll, but
  sometimes I would run,
For if a rabbit crossed my path I'd chase it just for
  fun.
I'd stop and chat with friends of mine, 'bout where
  the smells were best,
Until we had to move along, at his polite request.

But everything has changed and now we go at
  such a pace,
All our quiet, peaceful walks have turned into a
  race.
I'm losing all my friends because I haven't time to
  stop,
And when we get back to the house I only want
  to flop.
I'm hungry, thirsty, out of breath, and all my feet
  are throbbing;
The reason why? Well, can't you guess? My
  master's started jogging!

Marion Elliott

THE GOOD WIFE RELENTS

MY dear, I cannot tell
    How it could come about
That we, who loved so well,
Should turn to falling out,
But since the Spring is come
With running sap and leaves
Strong-shooting from the boughs,
And swallows in the eaves,
Since Spring is come with rain
To green and hidden ditches,
We'll mend the purse of love
With quick and purposed stitches.
Haste—April flies—
The winter bridge is down;
You must to the market
And I must to the town.

For you must buy a horse,
And a cow, and a cart,
And I must buy a quartern loaf
And half a gooseberry tart.
You must buy a rake
And a shovel and a hoe,
And I must buy some flowering chintz
And a bale of calico,
O and a rug with fringes
To spread along the floor,
And half an ounce of aniseed
And a handle for the door.
The gate is off its hinges,
The thatch is working down,
Hey, Love, to the market,
And ho, Love, to the town!

Gwen Clear

SUDDEN ENCOUNTER

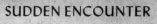

I ROSE from my lamplighted books,
    And went outside to darkness for an apple;
There I saw the new moon in the west,
Like a golden sickle.
The dog whined softly, so I turned aside
To set him free.
I heard an acorn tumble,
And wind in the tree.
Shutting the door of the apple-loft again,
I stared in silence idly at the moon,
A moment in a multitude of years.
My hand was at the latch of time unknown:
There, in delight I knew, but not how keen,
All my youth had quietly come again,
And quietly gone.

                        Frank Kendon

WINTER

NOW iron Winter holds the earth in thrall
　And ice transfixes every pool and pond,
The rooks fly low across the frosty fields
　To barren branches in the wood beyond.

The darkening sky enfolds the hedgerows round,
　A bronze sun lies at the land's bright rim,
The cattle stamp and sway in breathy byres,
　A silent owl sits waiting in the dim.

The first soft, sparkling flakes drift through the
　dark
　And over distant fells the clouds descend,
Fallow and silent sleeps the patient earth,
　Waiting the turn of the year, and Winter's end.

Betty Haworth

MONDAY STREET

DOWN into Monday Street one day
   Came a pedlar dancing in strange array;
With sandal shoes and a kingfisher's feather
And hands well used by wind and weather,
Came singing and bright and gay.

He sang as he pointed his sandalled feet
In Monday Street where the great men meet,
But the passers-by rubbed Monday's eyes
And shut them again in dim surprise,
Unaccustomed to songs so sweet.

He laughed with the load of his easy wares,
For he peddled no pack and wore no cares;
He offered a grin to the Monday folks
But Monday faces are not for jokes,
Being lengthened with grave affairs.

So he danced away out by the gasworks wall,
And no-one in Monday Street can recall
The song that was strange and gay and sweet
Or the turn of the sandals that stepped so neat
When the pedlar came—if he came at all.

John Jarmain

ENGLAND

NO lovelier hills than thine have laid
    My tired thoughts to rest;
No peace of lovelier valleys made
    Like peace within my breast.

Thine are the woods whereto my soul,
    Out of the noontide beam,
Flees for a refuge green and cool
    And tranquil as a dream.

Thy breaking seas like trumpets peal;
    Thy clouds—how oft have I
Watched their bright towers of silence steal
    Into infinity!

My heart within me faints to roam,
    In thought even far from thee;
Thine be the grave whereto I come,
    And thine my darkness be.

Walter de la Mare

PIANO PRACTICE

I WANT to play, I want to sing,
   The sun is out and I'm shut in,
And all because of this beastly thing
   They call piano practice.

Note after note, black after white
I plod for half an hour each night,
And all because I can't get it right.
   I hate piano practice.

My scales are rough, the notes are wrong,
I wait at bar-lines far too long,
Yet they still make me come along
   For more piano practice.

I'm going to run; I'm going to tease,
I'm going to do just what I please,
And I'll crash the lid down over the keys
   And skip piano practice.

Jacqueline Emery

WHEN MY SHIP COMES IN

WHAT shall I wear when my ship comes in?
　　Oh, I'll dress in satins and lace and silk,
In velvet and furs and soft doeskin,
　　And Puss shall have saucers of milk.

What shall I do when my ship ties up?
　　I'll put on my jewels, my rings of gold,
I'll drink sweet wine from a silver cup,
　　And Puss shall have mice from the hold.

Oh, how shall I spend the money that's mine
　　When my ship sails home from the seas?
On mortar and bricks and a builder's line,
　　And a basket for Puss, if you please!

And I'll build me a house when my ship comes
　　home
　　And my garden shall look like a dream,
And I'll share it with all who may care to come
　　And Puss I shall pamper with cream!

Mary M. Milne

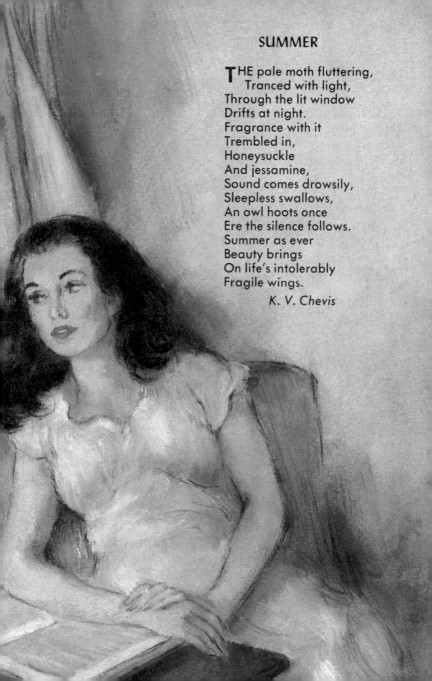

SUMMER

THE pale moth fluttering,
  Tranced with light,
Through the lit window
Drifts at night.
Fragrance with it
Trembled in,
Honeysuckle
And jessamine,
Sound comes drowsily,
Sleepless swallows,
An owl hoots once
Ere the silence follows.
Summer as ever
Beauty brings
On life's intolerably
Fragile wings.

K. V. Chevis

REDBIRDS

REDBIRDS, redbirds,
 Long and long ago,
What a honey-call you had
 In the hills I used to know;

Redbud, buckberry,
 Wild plum-tree,
And proud river sweeping
 Southward to the sea,

Brown and gold in the sun
 Sparkling far below,
Trailing stately round her bluffs
 Where the poplars grow—

Redbirds, redbirds,
 Are you singing still
As you sang one May day
 On Saxton's Hill?

Sara Teasdale

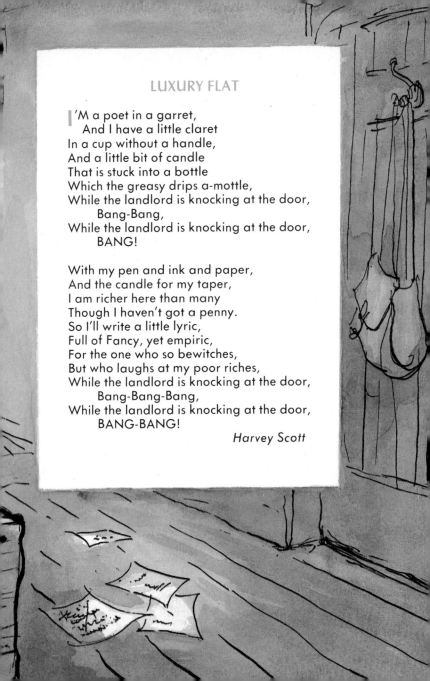

LUXURY FLAT

I'M a poet in a garret,
   And I have a little claret
In a cup without a handle,
And a little bit of candle
That is stuck into a bottle
Which the greasy drips a-mottle,
While the landlord is knocking at the door,
    Bang-Bang,
While the landlord is knocking at the door,
    BANG!

With my pen and ink and paper,
And the candle for my taper,
I am richer here than many
Though I haven't got a penny.
So I'll write a little lyric,
Full of Fancy, yet empiric,
For the one who so bewitches,
But who laughs at my poor riches,
While the landlord is knocking at the door,
    Bang-Bang-Bang,
While the landlord is knocking at the door,
    BANG-BANG!

Harvey Scott

MY LOVE

MY love is like the morning—
　　The first sweet light of day,
My love is like the dawning,
　　When night clouds drift away;
My love is like the first breath
　　That stirs the sleep-drenched air,
And when I greet the morning,
　　I see my loved one there.

My love is like the mid-day
　　When sun is warm and kind,
When soft airs fall around me
　　And soothe my troubled mind;
My love is like the birdsong
　　That fills the sunlit air,
And in the glow of noon-tide,
　　My love is waiting there.

My love is like the evening
　　When lights are soft and low—
When shadows fall before me
　　And fragrant night winds blow;
My love is like the first rays
　　When stars begin to peep
And weave their spell about me,
　　And sanctify my sleep.

Victorine Buttberg

THE PLAY-GROUP

JENNIFER sucking her thumb by the door;
  Anthony stamping his foot on the floor;
Matthew, surrounded by two or three more,
Trying to take off his shoes.

Kate holding tightly to Mummy's safe hand;
Philippa building a castle of sand;
Ben busy making his aeroplane land,
Right on Sebastian's toes.

Jonathan riding a bike round and round;
Tom in a corner not making a sound;
Angela clutching a doll that she's found,
Which hasn't, as yet, got a name.

Edward and Timothy kicking a ball;
Alison painting a picture with Paul;
William crying because of a fall
Over little Victoria's chair.

Everyone silent, a story is told—
A tale of adventure which never grows old.
Caroline shivers, but not from the cold.
How lovely it is to be three!

Marion Elliott

A MAY SONG

THE banners of the beech are out,
    The wildwood bands are playing;
And who would sit the fire about
    When all the vale's a-Maying?

Then up, let's take the footpath way,
    In house who will may burrow;
Fresh joys shall greet us all the day,
    From woodland, mead and furrow.

The throstle bugle leads the line,
    The blackbird is his fellow;
And crimson tassels deck the pine,
    That lordly violoncello.

The thorn hath donned a snow-white cloak,
    With carmine slashed and pointed;
And May hath touched the royal oak
    And every bough anointed.

The lambs flock to the cuckoo's call,
    Staid rooks bright plumes are sporting,
And wilding creatures, great and small,
    From morn till eve are courting.

Then up, let's take the footpath way,
    Through field and forest hie us;
Too soon the year and we shall grey,
    So let who dare deny us.

John S. Martin

THE CIRCUS PASSED TODAY

THE Circus came to town today,
   It passed us in the lane;
I've seen it many times, and yet
   Today was not the same.

Today I had a friend with me,
   A small, warm hand in mine,
A face transfixed with wonder
   And two bright eyes ashine.

We saw an elephant go by,
   A pony, white as milk,
A tiger with a golden eye
   And clowns in rainbow silk.

We stood there in the sunny lane
   And watched them all pass by,
The caravans, the acrobats,
   The glorious panoply.

A well-loved sight, and yet today
   Some magic seemed to shine;
Could it have been that joyful face,
   That small hand held in mine?

Betty Haworth

THE BEGINNING

THE shadowed woods loom dark and still
    Against the sky of grey and rose,
The last light lingers on the hill,
    The last bird slowly homeward goes.

This moment will not come again,
    The trees, the homing bird, the sky,
The dying gleam all down the lane
    Where we stand silent, you and I.

This is the instant, this the place
    Where love is born all unaware.
Our course is set, ahead we face
    The journey that is ours to share.

Mary C. Marshall

THE LAD'S LOVE BY THE GATE

DOWN in the dear West Country, there's a
   garden where I know
   The Spring is rioting this hour, though I am
   far away—
Where all the glad flower-faces are old loves of
   long ago,
   And each in its accustomed place is blossoming
   to-day.

The lilac drops her amethysts upon the mossy wall,
   While in her boughs a cheerful thrush is calling
   to his mate.
Dear breath of mignonette and stocks! I love you,
   know you all.
   And, oh, the fragrant spices from the lad's love
   by the gate!

Kind wind from the West Country, wet wind, but
   scented so,
   That straight from my dear garden you seem
   but lately come,
Just tell me of the yellow broom, the guelder rose's
   snow,
   And of the tangled clematis where myriad
   insects hum.

Oh, is there any heartsease left, or any rosemary?
   And in their own green solitudes, say, do the
   lilies wait?
I knew it! Gentle wind, but once—speak low and
   tenderly—
   How fares it—tell me truly—with the lad's love
   by the gate?

Fay Inchfawn

WINTER NIGHT

BEFORE the flickering fire my young dogs sleep,
    Pursuing, in their dreams, elusive prey;
Behind my chair long shadows quietly creep,
    And, on the shelves, old plates and dishes play
With dancing firelight. Pattering rain descends
    Upon the mullioned windows, but within,
The chimney's laughing luff with joy ascends
    To battle with bleak winter and to win
A man-made triumph with old griefs o'erthrown.
    There's peace beside the fire while sullen rain
And wind contrive to make the oak-trees groan,
    While, through the storm, upon the
      window-pane,
A rose-shoot taps soft answer from the night,
And, suddenly, my room is summer bright.

Harvey Scott

BALLAD OF JOHN SILVER

WE were schooner-rigged and rakish, with a
    long and lissome hull;
And we flew the pretty colours of the cross-bones
    and the skull;
We'd a big black Jolly Roger flapping grimly at
    the fore,
And we sailed the Spanish Water in the happy
    days of yore.

We'd a long brass gun amidships, like a well-
    conducted ship,
We had each a brace of pistols and a cutlass at
    the hip;
It's a point which tells against us, and a fact to be
    deplored,
But we chased the goodly merchant-men and laid
    their ships aboard.

O! the fiddle on the fo'c's'le, and the slapping
    naked soles,
And the genial "Down the middle, Jake, and
    curtsey when she rolls!"
With the silver seas around us and the pale moon
    overhead,
And the look-out not a-looking and his pipe-bowl
    glowing red.

Ah! the pig-tailed, quidding pirates and the pretty
    pranks we played,
All have since been put a stop-to by the naughty
    Board of Trade;
The schooners and the merry crews are laid away
    to rest,
A little south the sunset in the Islands of the Blest.

John Masefield

IRISH GIRL

I DREAM of Connemara
　Where the hills go ranging free,
And the little streams are laughing
　As they run to meet the sea.

Through my window in the city
　Come the noises of the street,
But oh, I treasure memories
　Of sounds more rare and sweet!

Rain hissing down the chimney
　Upon the smouldering peat,
The curlew's call across the moor,
　Clip-clop of donkey's feet;

The moan of wind on lonely shores,
　The wild waves in the bay,
The murmur from the chapel
　As the people kneel to pray.

And as the city darkness falls,
　A voice within me sings
The unforgotten songs that lift
　My heart on shining wings.

Margaret Bentley

AUTUMN SONG

NOW leafy winds are blowing cold,
    And south by west the sun goes
    down,
A quiet huddles up the fold
In sheltered corners of the brown.

Like scattered fire the wild fruit strews
The ground beneath the blowing tree,
And there the busy squirrel hews
His deep and secret granary.

And when the night comes starry clear,
The lonely quail complains beside
The glistening waters on the mere
Where widowed beauties yet abide.

And I, too, make my own complaint
Upon a reed I plucked in June,
And love to hear it echoed faint
Upon another heart in tune.

Francis Ledwidge

IN SOMERSET

IN Somerset they guide the plough
 From early dawn till twilight now.
The good red earth smells sweeter yet,
Behind the plough, in Somerset.
The celandines round last year's mow
Blaze out . . . and with his old-time vow
The south wind woos the violet,
In Somerset.

Then, every brimming dyke and trough
Is laughing wide with ripples now,
And oh, 'tis easy to forget
That wintry winds can sigh and sough,
When thrushes chant on every bough
In Somerset!

Fay Inchfawn

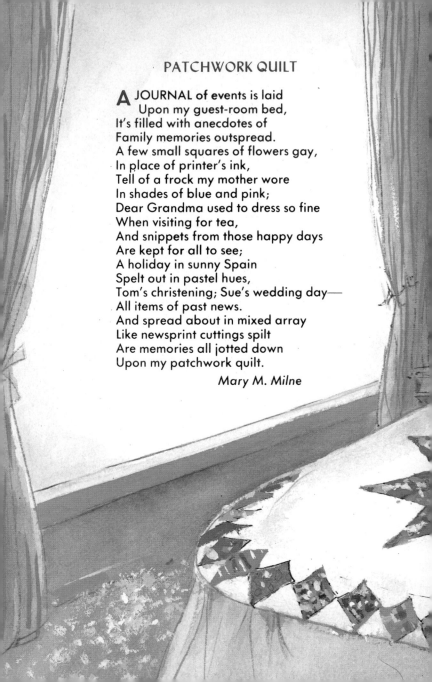

PATCHWORK QUILT

A JOURNAL of events is laid
   Upon my guest-room bed,
It's filled with anecdotes of
Family memories outspread.
A few small squares of flowers gay,
In place of printer's ink,
Tell of a frock my mother wore
In shades of blue and pink;
Dear Grandma used to dress so fine
When visiting for tea,
And snippets from those happy days
Are kept for all to see;
A holiday in sunny Spain
Spelt out in pastel hues,
Tom's christening; Sue's wedding day—
All items of past news.
And spread about in mixed array
Like newsprint cuttings spilt
Are memories all jotted down
Upon my patchwork quilt.

Mary M. Milne

LEAF FROM A FLY-BOOK

THE king's road is a troublous summons calling day and day;
But my feet take the cocksfoot track—the easy, vagrant way.
Beside the restless acres and the gold of noisy gorse,
The ripple lures its lover down the dazzle of its course.

Its speech is of the willow-reaches rich with lurking joy,
The revel of the rapids where gay life is death's decoy;
My heart is with the laughing lips; I follow up and down,
But follow not the king's white road toward the haste of town.

Afoot, the wash of waders, and aloft, the haze-veiled blue—
The heart it needeth nothing so the cast fall clean and true.
O carol of the running reed, O flash of mottled back!
And who will take the king's white road, and who the cocksfoot track?

The hour-glass fills with weather like a wine of
    slow content,
I throw the world behind me as a cartridge that is
    spent.
Then home by summer starlight bear my grass-
    cool, mottled load;
I quit the pleasant cocksfoot track: I take the king's
    white road.
                 Seaforth MacKenzie

A COUNTRY CHURCHYARD

HERE in my inner eye I hold
    The fragile image of a well loved scene.
Trees in high summer fullness, and the curling
    river,
    Low wooded hillside under a haze of green.

Above the river flats and garden plots
    Silent and candle cool the old church stands.
Slanting and mote-beamed sunlight
    Splashes on flowers placed by loving hands.

From His bright Eastern window Christ looks down
    Onto the gleaming chancel and the nave,
And in the silence hears a blackbird singing
    Upon the warm stone of an ancient grave.

Here in my inner eye I hold
    The precious image, and my heart yet swells
To a surprise of primroses, half hidden,
    A march of elms, and Sunday evening bells.

In stillness, and the slowly passing seasons,
    In birdsong and the wide oak shade,
Century after century unchanging,
    This holy place is ever holier made.

Betty Haworth

FARMER'S BOY

IT is a naked country without trees,
    Scourged by winds from the seas,
    Bald and bare;
Harsh with sounds that drive like stones through
    the air . . .
    They do say
There were forests here once on a day,
But the great wars stole them away.

And when I walk at noon up the bare,
The beaten ridge, where
    The grass grows,
Where once, they say, the pines climbed in rows,
    I do hear
A singing like to harps in my ear,
And like a ship at sea the wind goes.

                                    Rose Macaulay

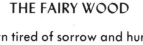

THE FAIRY WOOD

I HAVE grown tired of sorrow and human tears;
 Life is a dream in the night, a fear among fears,
A naked runner lost in a storm of spears.

I have grown tired of rapture and love's desire;
Love is a flaming heart, and its flames aspire
Till they cloud the soul in the smoke of a windy fire.

I would wash the dust of the world in a soft green
     flood;
Here between sea and sea in this fairy wood,
I have found a delicate wave-green solitude.

Here, in the fairy wood, between sea and sea,
I have heard the song of a fairy bird in a tree,
And that peace that is not in the world has flown
     to me.

Arthur Symons

LISTENING

HIS step? Ah, no; 'tis but the rain
   That hurtles on the window pane.
Let's draw the curtains close and sit
Beside the fire awhile and knit.
Two purl—two plain. A well-shaped sock,
And warm. (I thought I heard a knock,
But 'twas the slam of Jones's door.)
Yes, good Scotch yarn is far before
The fleecy wools—a different thing,
And best for wear. (Was that his ring?)
No. 'Tis the muffin man I see;
We'll have threepennyworth for tea.
Two plain—two purl; that heel is neat.
(I hear his step far down the street.)
Two purl—two plain. The sock can wait;
I'll make the tea. (He's at the gate!)

Fay Inchfawn

REMEMBER

BLUE . . .
    The bluebell woods we walked through,
The cloudless sky above;
The dress that you were wearing
That day we fell in love.

Blue . . .
The calm, unruffled water,
The mountains wreathed in mist,
The little boat we sailed in
That day when first we kissed.

Blue . . .
The flowers on the altar,
Two bridesmaids dressed the same;
Your eyes that shone so brightly
That day you took my name.

Blue . . .
The baby cards which welcome
Our first-born child, a boy;
The teddy bear I bought him
Today completes my joy.

Marion Elliott

APPLE FIRES

THE apples set the lofts alight
    With fires of red and gold; amidst the cold
White ways of winter, the harvest of the year
Flames through the frost-bound land,
And, standing here, within our apple loft,
I stretch my hand to the glowing fire,
And take an apple, round and ripe and red,
And feel the sun of summer on my head—
The sun that lit the apple fires to burn
In the dark barns, until, with his return,
New fires are started in the apple trees,
Of leaf and flower, fanned by the bustling breeze,
So that at length, they, too, shall gleam and glow
Within the barns, on days of frost and snow!

Aileen E. Passmore

MORNING SONG

THE thrush is in the wattle tree, an', " O, you pretty
    dear!"
He's callin' to his little wife for all the bush to hear.
He's wantin' all the bush to know about his charmin' hen;
He sings it over fifty times, an' then begins again.
For it's Mornin'! Mornin'! The world is wet with dew,
With tiny drops a-twinkle where the sun comes shinin' thro'.

Oh, it's good to be a wealthy man, it's grand to be a king
With mornin' on the forest-land an' joy in everything.
It's fine to be a healthy man with healthy work to do
In the singin' land, the clean land, washed again with dew.
When sunlight slants across the trees, an' birds begin to
    sing,
Then kings may snore in palaces, but I'm awake——and
    king.

But the king must cook his breakfast, an' the king must
    sweep the floor,
Then out with axe on shoulder to his kingdom at the door;
His old dog sportin' on ahead, his troubles all behind,
An' joy mixed in the blood of him because the world is kind.
For it's Mornin'! Mornin'! Time to out an' strive!
Oh, there's not a thing I'm askin' else but just to be alive!

C. J. Dennis

A PRAYER IN SPRING

OH, give us pleasure in the flowers today;
   And give us not to think so far away
As the uncertain harvest; keep us here
All simply in the springing of the year.

Oh, give us pleasure in the orchard white,
Like nothing else by day, like ghosts by night;
And make us happy in the happy bees,
The swarm dilating round the perfect trees.

And make us happy in the darting bird
That suddenly above the bees is heard,
The meteor that thrusts in with needle bill,
And off a blossom in mid air stands still.

For this is love and nothing else is love,
The which it is reserved for God above
To sanctify to what far ends He will,
But which it only needs that we fulfil.

Robert Frost

INVITATION

COME with me and I will show you,
   Where the cresses thickly grow,
How the little trout lie hidden
   In the shallows down below.

In my boat we'll go adrifting,
   Timelessly as in a dream,
Down the sequin-patterned highway
   Over haunts of perch and bream.

When the hour is ripe I'll bid you
   Share with me the mystic sight
Of the dragonflies' romancing
   Where they skim so swift and light.

Come with me and let me tell you
   All the river lore I know,
Of the life above the water,
   Of the silver fish below.

Hasten then that we may find them—
   Much to see and much to hear:
Birdsong, meadowsweet, wild roses,
   All are waiting, oh so near!

Violet Hall

IF ONLY—

IF only dinner cooked itself,
  And groceries grew upon the shelf;
If children did as they were told,
And never had a cough or cold;
And washed their hands, and wiped their boots,
And never tore their Sunday suits,
But always tidied up the floor,
Nor once forgot to shut the door.

If John remembered not to throw
His papers on the ground. And oh!
If he would put his pipes away,
And shake the ashes on the tray
Instead of on the floor close by;
And always spread his towel to dry,
And hung his hat upon the peg,
And never had bones in his leg.

Then, there's another thing. If Jane
Would put the matches back again
Just where she found them, it would be
A save of time for her and me.
And if she never did forget
To put the dustbin out; nor yet
Contrive to gossip with the baker,
Nor need ten thunderbolts to wake her.

Ahem! If wishes all came true,
I don't know what I'd find to do,
Because if no one made a mess
There'd be no need of cleanliness.
And things might work so blissfully,
In time—who knows?—they'd not need me!

And this being so, I fancy whether
I'll go on keeping things together.

Fay Inchfawn

ROWER'S CHANT

ROW till the land dip 'neath
     The sea from view.
Row till a land peep up,
     A home for you.

Row till the mast sings songs
     Welcome and sweet.
Row till the waves, outstripped,
     Give up, dead beat.

Row till the sea-nymphs rise
     To ask you why
Rowing you tarry not
     To hear them sigh.

Row till the stars grow bright
     Like certain eyes;
Row till the noon be high
     As hopes you prize.

Row till you harbour in
     All longing's port.
Row till you find all things
     For which you sought.

T. Sturge Moore

IT WAS A LOVER...

IT was a lover and his lass,
   With a hey, and a ho, and a hey nonino,
That o'er the green-cornfield did pass
   In the spring time, the only pretty ring time,
When birds do sing, hey ding a ding, ding:
Sweet lovers love the spring.

Between the acres of the rye,
   With a hey, and a ho, and a hey nonino,
These pretty country folks would lie,
   In the spring time, the only pretty ring time,
When birds do sing, hey ding a ding, ding:
Sweet lovers love the spring.

This carol they began that hour,
　　With a hey and a ho, and a hey nonino,
How that a life was but a flower
　　In the spring time, the only pretty ring time,
When birds do sing, hey ding a ding, ding:
Sweet lovers love the spring.

And therefore take the present time,
　　With a hey, and a ho, and a hey nonino;
For love is crowned with the prime
　　In spring time, the only pretty ring time,
When birds do sing, hey ding a ding, ding:
Sweet lovers love the spring.

William Shakespeare

VICTORIA JANE

IF ever I marry Victoria Jane,
  She'll have a fine house at the end of the lane;
A butler, a cook and a personal maid;
A Sheraton suite and a table that's laid
With cut glass and silver-ware, damask and lace,
And small printed cards that show everyone's
  place.

If ever I marry Victoria Jane,
She'll have many dresses, both patterned and
  plain;
And, made to the latest new fashion from France,
A satin ball-gown if she chooses to dance.
Her blue velvet cloak and her muff, lined with silk,
Shall have a fur trim just the colour of milk.

If ever I marry Victoria Jane,
She'll never get wet if it chances to rain;
A maid with a message shall quickly run down:
" My Lady is waiting and ready for town!"
The coachman will bring round her carriage and
  pair;
I'll always make sure she has never a care . . .
If ever I marry Victoria Jane!

Greta Aspland

A VAGABOND SONG

THERE is something in the Autumn that is native
    to my blood—
Touch of manner, hint of mood;
And my heart is like a rhyme,
With the yellow and the purple and the crimson
    keeping time.

The scarlet of the maples can shake me like a cry
Of bugles going by.
And my lonely spirit thrills
To see the frosty asters like smoke upon the hills.

There is something in October sets the gipsy blood
    astir;
We must rise and follow her,
When from every hill aflame
She calls and calls each vagabond by name.

Bliss Carman

THE STRAW HAT

SHE wore it on a summer day,
   When all the air was filled with may,
Sweet lilacs, honeysuckle, lime,
Gay new-mown hay, and pensive thyme.

With liquid blackbird, silvery wren,
The bold thrush sang his song again,
Alas, in vain, for all I saw
Was Janet in her hat of straw.

Its shade?—A golden-honey brown—
A tiny fringe of veil hung down—
Naive? Ah, no—demurely wise.
And oh, the beauty of her eyes!

I think I'd marry her tomorrow,
If I a decent suit could borrow,
And hear her solemn promise that
In church she'd wear that dear straw hat.

Harvey Scott

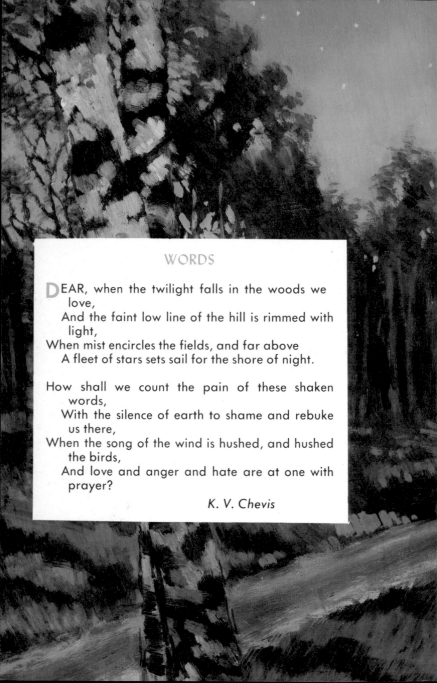

WORDS

DEAR, when the twilight falls in the woods we
    love,
    And the faint low line of the hill is rimmed with
    light,
When mist encircles the fields, and far above
    A fleet of stars sets sail for the shore of night.

How shall we count the pain of these shaken
    words,
    With the silence of earth to shame and rebuke
    us there,
When the song of the wind is hushed, and hushed
    the birds,
    And love and anger and hate are at one with
    prayer?

K. V. Chevis

TABLECLOTHS

AT breakfast time I love to see
    A gay cloth on the table laid,
Bright yellow cups to hold the tea,
A green pot for the marmalade.
So, if the morning should be grey,
A happy note still starts the day.

At tea time, though, I like to spread
A lacy cloth, for added grace.
Rose-patterned china will instead
The yellow crockery replace,
And bright a silver teapot shine
Upon this tablecloth of mine.

At picnic time my cloth is made
Of short-cropped grass and daisies bright,
With homely cups and plates arrayed,
And fruit to tempt the appetite.
In warmth of sun or cool of shade,
My tablecloth is nicely laid.

Winifred Williams

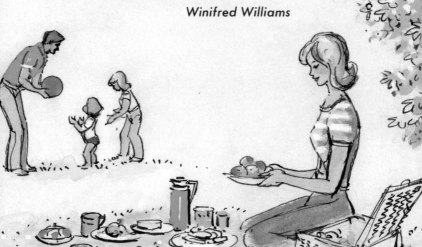

THE MILKMAID

ACROSS the grass I see her pass;
　　She comes with tripping pace—
A maid I know—and March winds blow
　　Her hair across her face;
With a hey, Dolly! ho, Dolly!
　　Dolly shall be mine,
Before the spray is white with may,
　　Or blooms the eglantine.

The March winds blow; I watch her go,
　　Her eye is brown and clear;
Her cheek is brown, and soft as down
　　(To those who see it near!)
With a hey, Dolly! ho, Dolly!
　　Dolly shall be mine,
Before the spray is white with may,
　　Or blooms the eglantine.

What has she not that those have got,
　　The dames that walk in silk?
If she undo her 'kerchief blue,
　　Her neck is white as milk.
With a hey, Dolly! ho, Dolly!
　　Dolly shall be mine,
Before the spray is white with may,
　　Or blooms the eglantine.

Break, break, to hear, O crocus-spear!
　　O tall Lent-lilies, flame!
There'll be a bride at Easter-time,
　　And Dolly is her name.
With a hey, Dolly! ho, Dolly!
　　Dolly shall be mine,
Before the spray is white with may,
　　Or blooms the eglantine.

Austin Dobson

LESSONS

WILLIAM THE CONQUEROR, Ten-Sixty-six—
    I know what I'll build after tea with my bricks!
I'll build a great castle with drawbridge and keep,
And arches through which I shall see, when I peep,
Saxon and Norman both up to their tricks . . .
William the Conqueror, Ten-Sixty-six.

Madrid is the Capital City of Spain—
I know what I'll do if it only won't rain!
I'll set my new boat in full sail on the lake,
Commanded by Hawkins and Raleigh and Drake,
To conquer the Spanish Armada again.
Madrid is the Capital City of Spain . . .

Eleanor Farjeon

THE WIND AND THE CORN

T HE wind to the standing corn,
Upon an August day—
When you were green, that now are ripe,
I kissed the Maid of May.
She had hawthorn petal shells
On her cap and gown;
But I came over Grasstop Hill
And blew the petals down.

In thirty days, or thirty-one,
About the first of June,
When you were ankle-deep and dark
Beneath a growing moon,

I stole softly here and there,
    Softly far and near;
In river meadow or Grasstop Hill
    I could not find my dear.

When you are reaped, that now be ripe,
    You will not feel the rain;
But I shall wake with new-year spring
    To find the Maid again.
Cherry petal shells she'll wear
    In her morning gown,
And I'll come over Grasstop Hill
    And shake the petals down—
        Down, down, down again,
        And shake the petals down!

Frank Kendon

SUMMER SONG

I LAID me to rest in the quiet dusk
   And I woke when the sun was high
To the purling flow of the whimbrels' song
   As it poured from the echoing sky.

It filled my ears with the voice of Summer,
   Lulled my heart with a moorland dream
That bore me along with the tranquil days
   On the bird-song's flowing stream.

Now I lay me to rest on a winter night
   Where the town wind mourns and cries,
But I'll dream again of the whimbrels' song
   And the cloudless moorland skies.

Mary C. Marshall

CHERRY RIPE

THERE is a garden in her face
    Where roses and white lilies blow;
A heavenly paradise in that place,
    Wherein all pleasant fruits do grow;
There cherries grow that none may buy,
Till Cherry-Ripe themselves do cry.

Those cherries fairly do enclose
    Of orient pearl a double row,
Which when her lovely laughter shows,
    They look like rose-buds filled with snow:
Yet them no peer nor prince may buy,
Till Cherry-Ripe themselves do cry.

Her eyes like angels watch them still;
    Her brows like bended bows do stand,
Threat'ning with piercing frowns to kill
    All that approach with eye or hand
These sacred cherries to come nigh,
Till Cherry-Ripe themselves do cry.

Anonymous

CIDER SONG

THE wine they drink in Paradise
    They make in Haute Lorraine;
God brought it burning from the sod
To be a sign and signal rod
That they that drink the blood of God
    Shall never thirst again.

The wine they praise in Paradise
    They make in Ponterey,
The purple wine of Paradise,
But we have better at the price;
It's wine they praise in Paradise,
    It's cider that they pray.

The wine they want in Paradise
    They find in Plodder's End,
The apple wine of Hereford,
Of Hafod Hill and Hereford,
Where woods went down to Hereford,
    And there I had a friend.

The soft feet of the blessed go
    In the soft western vales,
The road the silent saints accord,
The road from Heaven to Hereford,
Where the apple wood of Hereford
    Goes all the way to Wales.

                    G. K. Chesterton

BUDS

THE raining hour is done,
   And, threaded on the bough,
The may-buds in the sun
   Are shining emeralds now.

As transitory these
   As things of April will,
Yet, trembling in the trees,
   Is briefer beauty still.

For, flowering from the sky
   Upon an April day,
Are silver buds that lie
   Amid the buds of may.

The April emeralds now,
   While thrushes fill the lane,
Are linked along the bough
   With silver buds of rain.

And, straightly though to earth
   The buds of silver slip,
The green buds keep the mirth
   Of that companionship.

John Drinkwater

MY TRUE LOVE

MY true love hath my heart, and I have his,
 By just exchange one to the other given:
I hold his dear, and mine he cannot miss,
 There never was a better bargain driven:
My true love hath my heart, and I have his.

His heart in me, keeps him and me in one,
 My heart in him, his thought and senses guides;
He loves my heart for once it was his own,
 I cherish his, because in me it bides:
My true love hath my heart, and I have his.

Sir Philip Sidney

ACKNOWLEDGMENTS

Our thanks to the Society of Authors and the Literary Trustees of Walter de la Mare for *England*; to the Society of Authors as the Literary Representative of the Estate of John Masefield for *Ballad of John Silver*; to Ward Lock Ltd. for *Somerset, Listening, If Only* and *The Lad's Love by the Gate* by Fay Inchfawn; to Michael Joseph for *Lessons* by Eleanor Farjeon; to Sidgwick and Jackson Ltd. for *Buds* by John Drinkwater; to Charles Griffiths for *Apple Fires* by Aileen E. Passmore; to Mrs Celia Kendon for *Sudden Encounter* and *The Wind and the Corn* by Frank Kendon; to Marion Elliot for *Dog Days, The Playgroup* and *Remember*; to Mary M. Milne for *Patchwork Quilt* and *Summer Song*; to Harvey Scott for *Luxury Flat, Winter Night* and *The Straw Hat*; to Victorine Buttberg for *My Love*; to Mary C. Marshall for *The Beginning* and *Summer Song*; to Violet Hall for *Invitation;* to Greta Aspland for *Victoria Jane;* to Margaret Bentley for *Irish Girl*; to Betty Haworth for *The Circus Passed Today, Winter* and *A Country Churchyard*.